DREAM JOBS IN SPORTS EQUIPMENT DESIGN

TRACY BROWN HAMILTON

Rosen
YA
New York

For Caroline Bourgeot

Published in 2018 by The Rosen Publishing Group, Inc.
29 East 21st Street, New York, NY 10010

Library of Congress Cataloging-in-Publication Data

Names: Hamilton, Tracy Brown, author.
Title: Dream Jobs in Sports Equipment Design /
Tracy Brown Hamilton.
Description: New York : Rosen Publishing, 2018. | Series: Great Careers in the Sports Industry | Includes bibliographical references and index. | Audience: Grades 7–12.
Identifiers: LCCN 2017019522 | ISBN 9781538381403 (library bound) | ISBN 9781508178620 (paperback)
Subjects: LCSH: Sporting goods—Design and construction—Juvenile literature. | Sports—Vocational guidance—Juvenile literature.
Classification: LCC GV745 .H36 2018 | DDC 796.023—dc23
LC record available at https://lccn.loc.gov/2017019522

Manufactured in China

CONTENTS

INTRODUCTION

Albert Spalding appears here in his Boston Red Stockings uniform. He would later go on to revolutionize the baseball glove and create a sports equipment empire.

We often take for granted that the equipment we use today for various sports has always been a part of the game, but actually there are almost constant changes and upgrades to the types of equipment that is standard for various sports.

When we picture soccer equipment, most of us think of a standard-size ball, shin guards, and cleats. If you were to ask almost anyone today what equipment was needed to play baseball, that person would almost certainly say a bat, ball, and glove—but up until about 1870, only a bat and ball were used to play America's favorite pastime.

In 1877, Albert Spalding—the pitcher at the time for an early professional, now defunct, baseball team called the Boston Red Stockings—walked onto the field wearing a fingerless, padded leather glove. It caused a bit of a stir because it was not what was usually worn at the time. In modern baseball, this glove would have only been surprising because it did not cover the fingers, but in Spalding's time it was a very new thing to wear a glove at all.

Players at the time simply endured injuries they suffered by catching the ball with their bare hands— that is, until the glove finally became a standard piece of equipment. But even the first gloves worn in baseball were not what we picture or use today. Back then, pieces of leather were simply stitched together and stretched over the hand of the player. There was usually no padding to the glove and, as with Spalding's self-made glove, some had only some or even no fingers covered, leaving the rest exposed.

As the wearing of gloves became more mainstream in baseball, the relatively new piece of equipment needed to be standardized—meaning, rules and specifications had to be agreed upon as to how the gloves were to be made, their size, and so on. The National League and American Association had to come up with formal specifications as they do for all equipment used in professional baseball. In 1895, they determined that "the catcher and the first baseman are permitted to wear a glove or mitt of any size, shape or weight. All other players are restricted to the use of a glove or mitt weighing not over ten ounces, and measuring in circumference around the palm of the hand not over fourteen inches."

As with all pieces of sporting equipment, the gear used to play baseball evolved and improved over time, sometimes for protection—as with the baseball glove—but also to improve athletic performance—as with the change from heavier wooden bats to lighter bats that players can swing faster. Even the ball has changed, as we will see later in this resource.

Equipment can refer to anything from artificial turf on a football field to sports clothing that can help cool the body of an athlete, so it's a very broad term. Today, sports equipment is a major industry, making it an interesting and exciting career choice, ideal for creative problem solvers and lovers of sports. In fact, Albert Spalding himself went on to cofound A.G. Spalding, now known just as Spalding, a sporting goods company that specializes in designing balls for sports. But how sports equipment is designed has become far more scientific and research-based than back in the time when individual players would create their own gloves from strips of leather.

These days, sport equipment designers are scientists—usually engineers—who specialize in designing, testing, and improving all types of sports equipment and the materials used to create them. They also tend to be sports fanatics, with knowledge of various games, if not a passion for a specific one. It is a profession that attracts people with an appetite for both science and athletics. These people want to improve not only how safe and high performing an athlete or piece of equipment can be, but who sometimes design new ways that a game can be played with the introduction of new equipment.

Sports equipment has evolved over time, there is always room for improvement and innovation. That's what the exciting field of sports equipment design is all about. This book describes the innovations that sports equipment designers have already accomplished through the history of professional sports, as well as the different types of work professionals who fall under the title of sports equipment design actually do. It also explains how best to put yourself on track for a job in this exciting field, starting as early as middle or high school.

Chapter 1

WHAT EXACTLY DOES A SPORTS EQUIPMENT DESIGNER DO?

Sports equipment designers are also sometimes called sports engineers. They are tasked with applying their knowledge of math, physics, biology, and other disciplines to creating solutions or finding room for improvement in sports equipment design and development. This can mean designing equipment, building facilities, analyzing an athlete's performance, regulating standards, ensuring safety requirements are met, or developing coaching tools.

A sports equipment designer works to improve the safety and performance of all levels and types of sporting-related gear—and also on looking at the mechanics of how athletes interact with the equipment they use. This includes equipment used by professional or college athletes, as well as the equipment you see in a public gymnasium or what you might use when going for a run or riding your skateboard or bicycle. All of these things are carefully designed based on scientific research and testing to ensure they are safe

Much of the sports and recreational equipment you use and enjoy regularly has been designed by scientists, and is continually refined.

and perform to the best capacity.

There is no single job description for a sports equipment designer; the job itself encompasses many different functions. Some equipment designers work in labs developing lighter-weight materials for racing bikes, others work with multinational sporting manufacturers like Nike to design and test new running shoes that will prevent injury and increase a runner's speed.

Others work directly with people to assess how the human body functions during physical activity, such as how much oxygen one uses when climbing a steep hill on a racing bike or which muscles are used the most when sprinting. This knowledge helps inform sports engineers in how to create technology that helps athletes gather this data and analyze it to improve how they use their muscles and move their body to maximize their results.

Sports engineering or equipment design is about improving performance and safety through the development of new tools for training and participating in an athletic activity, but within that definition are many different areas of focus you can choose from. This chapter looks at all the various functions that fall under the title of sports engineering design.

FROM THE SMALLEST STITCH TO THE FASTEST YACHT, IT'S ALL ABOUT DESIGN

When you think sports equipment, you might think of obvious things like batting cages, weight machines, or golf clubs. But it actually involves a lot more than the actual equipment you use to play a sport.

Sports equipment includes safety equipment, like hockey masks, as well as the surface on which a sport is played. As an example, tennis can be played on clay courts, hard courts, grass courts, and carpet courts. The designers also have to consider the types of materials that are used to create or develop these things and how to put the various components together— the creation of glues and other substances to hold, for example, a hockey stick or other hi-tech piece of equipment together.

The types of sports equipment that exist are as broad as the sports they are designed to be used in. Regardless of the sport or game a piece of equipment is designed for, the process is a careful and informed one, with every detail examined and tested and continuously revisited to ensure the most effective design and materials are being used.

Because new developments occur all the time, there is constant change in sports equipment. In some cases, these new developments have come from other fields of science, such as the use of lightweight materials that were developed in the aerospace field and have been used to make equipment, from skis to bicycles, lighter.

Some of the changes seem more minor, but have had great impact. The design of the baseball, for example, has gone through enormous evolution over time. Before 1876, when A. G. Spalding designed the first league-standard ball, pitchers made their own balls, which meant they varied in size and weight, and they were far softer than the balls we use today. The older ones were basically string balls covered in leather, and they behaved very differently from the balls we use today.

The Spalding ball had rubber at its core, which was to the batter's disadvantage because it was difficult

Much of the sports equipment we take for granted now—such as the goalie helmet in hockey—actually was revolutionary at some point.

to hit that ball very far. It was this ball that was used during what is known as the dead-ball era, when there were far fewer runs scored in each game. Instead of power hitters like Babe Ruth knocking the ball out of the park for a home run, the game was one of strategy, of stealing bases to earn runs.

A new ball was premiered during the 1910 World Series. The new ball had cork, rather than rubber, in its center and that brought in a new era of higher-scoring games and stronger at bats.

During World War II, because of a rubber shortage, the baseball was changed temporarily to what was known as the balata ball. It was made from the dried sap of the balata tree, which is used as a substitute for rubber, but the ball did not act the same as its rubber cousin and led to far fewer home runs and runs scored than the rubber-core ball did. In a 1985 *Sports Illustrated* column, Noel Hynd recalled his father's memory of the wartime ball:

"Although I'm too young to remember baseball the way it was played in the spring of 1943, my father used to tell me about it. That was the year the major leagues opened the season with something called a 'balata' ball. In fact, balata ball was one of the nicer things the players called it.

It was round and white and had the familiar, reassuring Spalding label, but it sure didn't act like an ordinary baseball. It did bounce, but not very much, and that was the problem. For the first two weeks of the season, a gruesome specter haunted the game: Modern baseball appeared to be on its way back to the pre-1920 dead-ball era. The national pastime, as happens at regular intervals, was imperiled."

Even the small stitching of a baseball has been changed over time to improve performance. In the 2015 college baseball season, for the first time in 155 years, a flat-seamed (versus raised) ball was used. The decision was made after several months of testing at Washington State University in 2013. Researchers found that flat-seamed balls travel farther than raised-seamed ones, which slow down the longer they travel.

On the other end of the size spectrum, yacht design is taught as a course for mechanical engineering students at the Massachusetts Institute of Technology (MIT). Computer-aided design (CAD) is used to create various parts of a yacht to enhance performance, including the hull, appendages, and deck.

In the sport of yacht racing, the America's Cup is the main event. The 165-year-old event has seen near-constant changes in the sport, mainly because of scientific design changes. These innovations, according to TheVerge.com, "is not for looks, but to maximize aerodynamics, giving them the supernatural ability to skip along the water like a school of feasting barracudas."

The racing boats in the America's Cup are massive—they are 72 feet (22 meters) long with masts higher than 130 feet (40 m). The boats are engineered to be very light—around 13,000 pounds (5,897 kilograms)—which makes them extremely fast. Their sails are made of a strong material—not canvas as with other sailing boats—that can generate up to 7 tons (6 metric tonnes) of force. It takes a lot of scientific and engineering knowledge to design such boats, as their high speeds can make them very dangerous to maneuver and a design flaw can be deadly.

A SOCCER BALL WITH A MIND OF ITS OWN

Each time the World Cup soccer tournament is held—every four years—a new ball is designed for the event. During the 2010 World Cup, which was held in South Africa, a new ball was designed by Adidas, which soon became very controversial.

The so-called Jabulani ball came under fire when goalkeepers in particular complained that the behavior of the ball in the air was completely unpredictable. When a goalie error lead to the United States scoring against England during the cup, the ball was quickly blamed.

England manager Fabio Capello called the ball the worst he had ever seen. "For the players it is terrible," he told the British press. "It is also terrible for the keepers because it is impossible to anticipate the trajectory."

Even the press was unimpressed. BBC sports editor David Bond called the 2010 tournament "the most boring World Cup in history" and cited the ball as the cause. "Most people seem to be pointing the finger of blame at the swerving Jabulani," he wrote on his blog.

Adam Harland was a designer and a member of the department that developed and tested prototypes of the ball. He was personally brought under fire from fans and players but defended the design—the roundest soccer ball ever, as he called it.

"I do feel some of the criticism has been unfair," he told the Daily Mail. *"When I watched the opening games I was a bag of nerves. For the first 20 minutes I just kept watching the ball and couldn't absorb the game."* But he stood by the design. *"I'm pleased, and relieved, at what I've seen so far,"* he said. *"I think the ball has performed well. Maybe now the World Cup is under way the criticism will stop."*

The 2017 defending America's Cup champions, the Oracle team, worked with Airbus—manufacturer of aircraft—to design their latest sailing boat. To test how well the boat could withstand pressure, Airbus's extensive testing facilities were used to test the boat's fins under extreme stress.

This kind of testing is important because making a misjudgment can be deadly with this kind of equipment. According to *Wired* magazine, "These vessels are like luxury yachts the way Formula 1 cars are like family sedans: They drive, and the similarities stop there. The folks eager to win sailing's greatest prize sink fortunes on the latest modern technology and materials, yielding vessels that don't so much plow through the water as fly above it."

DEVELOPING NEW MATERIAL

Sports equipment encompasses not only what the athletes compete with, but also what they wear. When it comes to performance, every little detail can enhance or hinder. It can come down to the weight of your tennis racquet or the moisture your uniform absorbs as you sweat.

As speed is a major priority for many athletes—be they sprinters, swimmers, cyclists, or football players—the development of athletic garments is a fundamental aspect of athletic performance. There have been many developments made in this area over the years, for both professional and amateur athletes.

Serena Williams is one of the most powerful and recognized figures in professional tennis today. Thirty years ago the equipment she uses and surface she plays on were quite different.

Factors that can impact how aerodynamic a garment is—meaning garments with as little "drag" as possible caused by wind passing by—include the speed at which the athlete is moving, the body position, the fabric itself, and how the garment is put together. A proper fit is also important.

A fabric and the elements holding a garment together—zippers, for example—have been tested using wind tunnels to determine how much drag it has. This helps inform the development of garments for cyclists. In 2013, the British cycling team wore a new piece of clothing that was developed, with ridges and an aerodynamic helmet that had an air duct in it, which scientists believed would give the team and edge over the competition. What an athlete wears can have a direct impact on how he or she performs, and it is sport scientists and equipment designers who are responsible for identifying problem areas and finding solutions to them.

How a fabric reacts to moisture also impacts athletic performance. In 2014, Davide Filingeri, a PhD student at Loughborough University in England, did research to assess how moisture on the body affects athletes. What he found was that wetness on the skin is more irritating in certain areas of the body than others, particularly the lower back.

HOW DIFFERENT FABRICS FOR SPORTS CLOTHING COMPARE

With new fabric appearing on the market all the time, what type of garment is best for what kind of activity? How one garment moves, breathes, deals with sweat and water, and even smells compared to another can vary greatly. Here is how some of the most common athletic-gear fabrics compare.

Bamboo. This may come as a surprise, but bamboo—a tall, woody grass—can be pulped and used to make a natural fabric. According to performance designer Sarah Chase, it "feels insanely soft, repels odors, regulates your temperature, and is UPF 50+."

Cotton. Cotton is another natural fabric that can perform quite well in some activities, such as yoga, but because it absorbs water it can be very cumbersome to wear in a higher-impact activity, like running or spinning.

Gore-Tex. Gore-Tex is a synthetic substance that is coated on other fabrics to make them waterproof and windproof. It helps protect athletes from the elements while allowing the skin to breathe.

Nylon. Nylon is a fabric used in many types of athletic wear. It is stretchy and breathable and helps draw sweat and moisture away from the skin.

Polyester. This man-made cloth has many benefits for athletic performance: it's light, it breathes, and it does not absorb moisture. Its one downside is it traps odors more than natural fabrics.

(continued on the next page)

(continued from the previous page)

Polypropylene. This fabric is also made from plastic, similar to polyester. But unlike polyester, it is waterproof. According to Lauren Hallworth, product line manager for Brooks Running apparel, "Even if you're sweaty after a run and the outside of the shirt is wet, what's touching you is completely dry," says Hallworth. "It's great as a base layer."

Spandex. Spandex is often called Lycra, which is the brand name of this hyperstretchy fabric. It can stretch to nearly 600 percent of its size.

Filingeri conducted his research in order to inform a sports garment manufacturer on how to make better-performing clothing for athletes. "If we know that the lower back is more sensitive to skin wetness, and that that is something people don't like, we need to target that region of the body," Filingeri said. "We want to ensure there won't be a lot of wetness there so we might, for example, use a material in that area of shirts that has less insulation and is more air permeable, so the sweat will evaporate and not accumulate there. That way we reduce the amount of discomfort."

PROTOTYPING AND TESTING

A big part of the job of sports equipment designers and sports scientists is testing their theories of what equipment might work best and how much force or wear it can withstand. This is why it is important to have a scientific mind: A passion for coming up with and testing theories and continually refining until you get the result you are hoping to get is essential.

When a piece of equipment or clothing is being designed, prototyping (the creation of a sample of the item) and testing is an essential part of the process. Because equipment and garment design can be an expensive undertaking, computer technology is very useful in the creation of new equipment or clothing.

The desire for increased performance in all sports drives equipment manufacturers to want to develop lighter and more effective materials. Because this is such a competitive marketplace, sports equipment engineers are in demand to come up with new and innovative ways to bring to market the best products that give the most measurable results. Testing the effectiveness of these materials is key to ensuring continued innovation and discovery in the design of sports equipment.

If you are someone who is interested in thinking outside of the box, in borrowing ideas from other

Sport equipment manufacturers test all of their products in testing centers such as this one, where a runner is wearing sensors to test Adidas products in Germany.

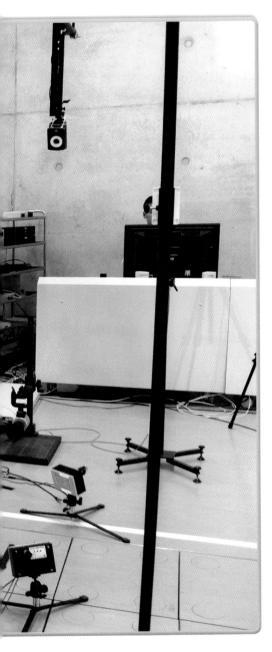

areas to apply them in a way that has not been done before, then you are innovative. Innovation can be inspired from anything. Last year, automobile manufacturer BMW got into the sports equipment design arena by creating a running shoe based on the design of one of its cars. "The approach was to look at every aspect of making a shoe and try to reimagine it," said senior vice president of BMW Group Design, Adrian van Hooydonk in a press release. "Freeing yourself of what is here now can be an enjoyable and rewarding exercise, typically it also speeds up change."

Technology such as 3D printing—the process of "printing" a three-dimensional object by layering thin strips of material on top of each other—is making prototyping sports equipment, from making shin guards to full body scans, of an athlete for testing purposes possible. Other technology such as computer-aided design (CAD) is also used in designing new sports equipment and inventing new technology for use in manufacturing.

CAD has completely changed the way manufacturers design new products, from sports equipment to airplanes. Before this technology became available, designers had to rely on simpler tools, such as pencils and compasses, to draft their ideas. CAD was originally developed in the 1960s for the manufacturing of automobiles.

Testing labs exist for the sole purpose of creating prototypes and testing them, to see how they withstand the elements, how they improve performance, how the athlete will interact with the equipment, and how it stands up to stress tests. Anything from a running shoe to a baseball bat to a bathing suit is put through such tests before a final design and product is ready for mass production. Using a testing lab enables a designer or engineer to see a 3D model of the design and even rotate it and and magnify it to get a better sense of how it will work in "real life." Familiarizing yourself with this kind of technology is a good idea if you are looking for a career in engineering, including, of course, in sports equipment design.

THE HUMAN FACTOR: ENSURING EQUIPMENT IS SAFE TO USE

Sports equipment designers must also know a lot about the human body, as it is a crucial element of the design process that equipment be safe to prevent injury. Some sports engineers work with athletes to make sure equipment is being used properly, as well as rehabilitation patients or nonprofessional athletes who deal with equipment designed for use by the general public.

From bobsleds to sailboats, a piece of equipment, once in the hands of a human being, can perform differently. The amount of weight or force applied, for one, can change how well or how safely a piece of equipment behaves. Sports equipment users from professional athletes to amateurs are involved in testing equipment to observe how it is used outside of the lab in the real world and to look for any design flaws that may be revealed by such testing.

For professional athletes, customizing equipment to ensure peak equipment and athlete interaction is also an important undertaking. The weight of a golf club or the height of a bike seat can have a big influence on performance outcome.

Sports equipment designers not only make equipment that leads to better performance, but that keeps its users safe—from badminton players to bobsledders.

Preventing injury to the athlete is a major concern. In 1969, the National Operating Committee on Standards for Athletic Equipment (NOCSAE) was created to establish standards and certification for athletic equipment by researching and testing equipment, developing new standards, and improving existing ones.

SPORTS AND EXERCISE MEDICINE

Sports engineering is separate from but related in many ways to sports medicine, or sports and exercise medicine (SEM), as it is known. This is a branch of medicine that deals with physical fitness and the

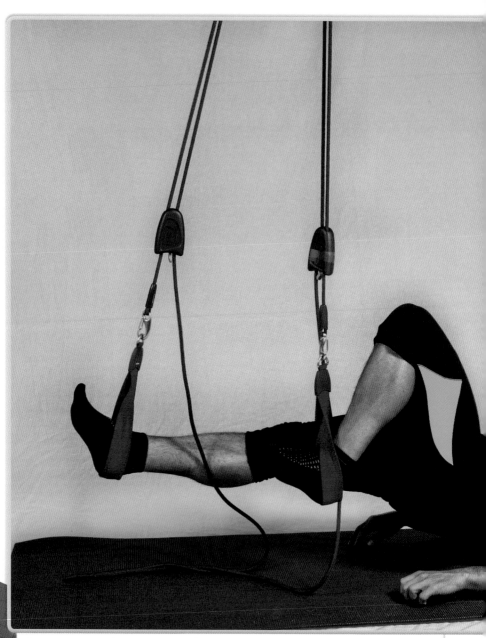

Sports equipment designers not only focus on creating tools for athletes to use for play, but also on developing products to help rehabilitate those with injuries.

treatment and prevention of injuries related to sports and exercise.

Like sports engineering, sports medicine is a broad field, which includes many specializations. The most traditional sports medicine professional works to help people heal, or rehabilitate, after an injury. This can mean treating injuries to bones, ligaments (tissue that connects bones or holds a joint together), or muscles.

Sports medicine professionals try to correct problems without surgery, instead relying on therapeutic massage, medication, devices, or exercises. For such exercises, equipment must also be designed with the specific purpose of helping an athlete repair damage caused by an injury.

Special physical therapy equipment is designed to help a person recover from an injury while also rebuilding strength. In order to design and use such equipment, the engineer and the sports medicine professional must understand how the patient will use the equipment and how to ensure it solves the problem rather than makes an injury even worse.

Examples of such special equipment include what is called a redcord. Physical therapist Ian Kornbluth describes it as "a suspension-based therapy system that leverages body weight as resistance and 'activates' dormant [inactive] muscles with high levels of neuromuscular [relating to nerves] stimulation. Redcord exercises require patients to use many muscles at the same time to keep the ropes steady. Meanwhile, slings and bungees stabilize weight and stress, enabling patients of all ages to exercise with proper form and without pain."

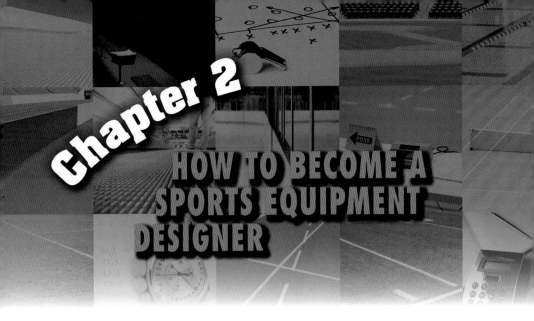

Chapter 2

HOW TO BECOME A SPORTS EQUIPMENT DESIGNER

Sports equipment design is an exciting career choice for anyone who loves sports and is interested in exploring the various ways performance can be enhanced through the development of new materials and innovative equipment revisions or inventions. However, it's a very competitive field and one that relies more on scientific knowledge and curiosity than a passion for a sport or sports in general. You can help prepare yourself, however, for a career in this field as early as middle school, by understanding what skills are needed and how they can be refined early on.

Unlike other careers, sports equipment design is a combination of a range of skills, including those in math, biology, and engineering. Being knowledgeable and skilled in these subjects can make you an ideal candidate for a job as a sports equipment designer and honing them early is a very good idea.

Having an interest or even a talent for athletics can help you toward a career in equipment design, but mostly it comes down to science.

Although there are university-level courses in the United Kingdom and elsewhere that focus specifically on sports design, they are not common, so the path to becoming a sports equipment designer may feel a little vague. In this section, we explore how you can best prepare yourself to have the skills it takes to succeed in this highly competitive, endlessly interesting field.

YOU LOVE SPORTS. HOW ABOUT SCIENCE?

If you want to go into the world of sports equipment design, you are likely to have more than a passing interest in athletics. Perhaps you are a great athlete yourself, or maybe you prefer

SOME DESIGNERS AND THEIR WORK

Writing for the Personal Trainer Development Center, Jonathan interviewed several people who had successfully designed and marketed their own equipment for use in public gymnasiums. Here is some advice from people who have managed to take their ideas and not only bring them to life but market them successfully.

The Ultimate Sandbag: Josh Herkin was a strength coach (a trainer who focuses on improving the strength of an athlete) before he invented the Ultimate Sandbag, a strength-training tool that claims to reduce injury. Herkin's advice for marketing new sports equipment is to focus on the benefits it can provide. "While features of the product are important," he says, "the marketplace is so saturated with equipment inevitably you have to show people 'why should I use your product?'"

The Lebert Equalizer: Mark Lebert is the designer behind this system of workout tools consisting of bars and straps. His advice is to find the right business partner. "I met with a business man who would soon become my partner," he says. "I knew his wife (an aerobics instructor) and son (taught him boxing) and he liked the idea, but the clincher was that his wife liked it. Being in the fitness industry, she saw that the Equalizers would have some widespread appeal and use."

The Core Tex: Anthony Carey created the Core Tex, a tool for what he calls "reactive training," a focus on movement and balance. "My advice is to make a prototype that gives proof of concept," he says. "Find people in your target market and those with industry experience willing to give you feedback."

to participate from the sidelines. In any case, while a love and understanding of sports would certainly make the sports equipment design field more fulfilling and satisfying to you, these are not the main requirements.

To be successful in this highly competitive field, it's crucial that you be passionate about science and technology. Thinking like a scientist is absolutely fundamental: You need to be someone who likes to solve problems and refine systems based on evidence and data arrived at through endless testing and refining and going back to the drawing board.

For one thing, you are likely to spend more of your time as a sports equipment engineer in a lab or at a computer than you are on a sports field, although some

As a sports equipment designer, you may work on anything from the smallest ping-pong ball to the highest ski jumping ramp.

members of the profession do work outside the walls of a lab or university. You might be working on equipment anywhere from ski jumping ramps to the golf course.

Whether you are working directly with athletes, creating a new all-weather running shoe, or researching the best fabric for cycling shorts, it is crucial that you have a curious, scientific mind, a passion for research and testing, and knowledge of not just engineering and computer skills but also an understanding of the human body and how it moves and works.

Dr. David James is a senior research fellow at the Center for Sports Engineering Research, Sheffield Hallam University in the United Kingdom who agrees that science comes first. "In my experience," he writes on sportsengineering.com, "employers look for engineering skill first and knowledge of sport thereafter. This is somewhat obvious, but alas many individuals assume that just because they love sport they have the necessary attributes to become a successful sports engineer. The reality is that sport is a competitive business and just as companies will look to the best athletes to endorse their products, they will also look to the best engineers to conduct research and development."

It is, of course, a benefit if you are passionate about a particular sport as well. That kind of interest and knowledge means you are familiar with the demands on the athlete and the equipment used and perhaps have some ideas for how to improve the performance of both. But overall, a desire for a career in a scientific field is by far more necessary to succeeding as a sports equipment designer.

SKILLS TO DEVELOP
BEFORE YOU GRADUATE

Much of succeeding as a sports equipment designer relies on the same skills that any other type of engineer requires. You can start developing these by applying them to other areas of academics and life, even if not directly related to sports.

HOW MATT NURSE GOT HIS DREAM JOB

Matt Nurse is the senior director at the Nike Sport Research Lab. In this role, he leads a multidisciplinary team of researchers, scientists, and innovators focused on biomechanics, human physiology, sensory perception, and data science.

Nurse has a PhD in biomechanics and medical science. He spoke with Designboom.com about how he landed his job with Nike and why he initially resisted accepting the position.

"[While studying] at the University of Calgary in Canada, [...] I worked in the human performance lab at the university, where we did a lot of research for sports equipment manufacturers," he says. "The international community of people who do this kind of work is only about 200–250 people so you get to know at least 70% of that community quite quickly. My predecessor at Nike, Mario LaFortune had approached me a few times to work with him, and initially I had doubts because I saw myself more as an academic who wanted to work at a university rather than a researcher at a company. Just prior to joining Nike, I was researching cleats for children and Mario explained to me that if I were to do the same kind of work at Nike, who would produce over 12 million cleats in the next five years, I would have a bigger impact on reducing injuries in the real world. The point was, that even if we only reduced injuries in 1% of the kids, that was still a massive, direct impact. This direct connection to results appealed to me and so I decided to join Nike."

(continued on page 45)

If you are someone who enjoys conducting research and testing different ideas until you find a solution, sports equipment design is a challenging, satisfying job.

(continued from page 43)

It was the right decision. "When I came to Nike, the big change was that I could immediately test research with the aid of prototypes and that certainly led to a deeper level of understanding," he says. "Before I joined Nike, I had the concern that I would just have to follow the plans of the company and that someone above me would guide all my research, but I couldn't have been more wrong. It's been very liberating. There's a very fresh, entrepreneurial spirit running through this huge company."

STEM skills (science, technology, engineering, and math) are key, as is the ability to work together with a team. Engineers are more often than not working with colleagues on projects.

Having a strong analytical mind is also a big benefit. This means you are curious about how things work and enjoy looking for cause and effect relationships and solutions to problems or possibilities for improvement. So much of sports engineering design is trial and error, testing, and experimenting.

There are other more general skills—good communication skills, for example, and the ability to discuss technical topics in a clear way—that will help you succeed. Computer experience, such as with design software, will also be useful to develop early on.

Even at the junior high and high school level, a focus on science and technology will help prepare you for a career in sports equipment design. Take as many such courses as you can, and join any after-school programs that focus on these subjects.

THE COURSES THAT ENSURE THE GREATEST SUCCESS

What courses you can start taking in junior or high school in order to prepare you for a career in sports equipment design or a college-level study in engineering depends on what is available to you at your school.

Taking all the math and science courses you can is definitely a good idea, and aiming to take higher-level, advanced placement courses in these areas is also smart. If your school also offers any kind of after-school program in computers or science, you should look into those as well.

According to college admissions expert Marjorie Hansen Shaevitz, in high school you should take the following courses in order to prepare yourself to apply to a university program that can lead to a career in sports equipment design:

Four years of math: Algebra II, trigonometry, pre-calculus, calculus, and even statistics

At least three years of science, including biology, chemistry, physics, with labs

Any computer science or engineering courses offered at your high school

Four years of English

Two to three years of a foreign language

Two years of social studies

In a Huffington Post blog piece, Shaevitz also warned that future engineering majors at the college level should expect to work very hard. "First of all, let me re-emphasize that engineering is the last thing you should think about if you are looking for a 'party-school major,' she says. Starting freshman year, engineering students usually take 18 units of hard science every quarter/semester

To prepare for a career in sports equipment design, it's a good idea to speak with your school counselor to focus on courses that will best help prepare you.

of their undergraduate career. It is a very structured, extremely rigorous area of study. Depending on individual colleges, most students complete their engineering degrees in four years plus a semester, but sometimes it takes five years."

COMMUNICATION SKILLS

There are few professions in which having strong communication skills is not a big advantage, and this is also true for sports equipment designers and all types of engineers in general.

Communicating well means listening and ensuring that you understand what is being said or otherwise communicated to you. This is important when working in teams and problem solving, as well as understanding the needs of your client or employer.

Good communication also means watching how you express yourself without words. Body language gives away a lot of information that you may not think is obvious. Knowing how to use eye contact, hand gestures, and posture to be sure you are expressing the right message is important.

Being clear and concise, getting to the point clearly in as few words as possible, is fundamental when working in teams, working with clients, and conducting scientific testing and experiments.

Being able to clearly understand and express ideas with others is especially important for engineers

Math, physics, engineering, and even interpersonal communication are the types of skills that can help open the door for you to a career in sports equipment design.

who work together to solve problems and invent new innovative solutions.

It's so important, in fact, that the engineering department at the University of Toronto, Canada, offers a special engineering communication program (ECP). It focuses on helping engineering students develop the writing, speaking, and critical-thinking skills that will be necessary for them to succeed in their careers.

In explaining why communication skills are so important to engineering students, the ECP director Deborah Tihanyi says, "the volume of writing that is required during an engineering degree often surprises students, but effective communication is also vital for success in the real world.

"Engineering is a multidisciplinary profession. A single project may involve teamwork with business specialists, psychologists and public health officials, to name a few. The ability to collaborate and communicate effectively with a diverse team, as well as express complex concepts to a non-technical audience, is an asset.

ECP helps students develop into proficient writers, speakers and communicators, both in print and online. More than ever, these skills are vital to engineering leaders."

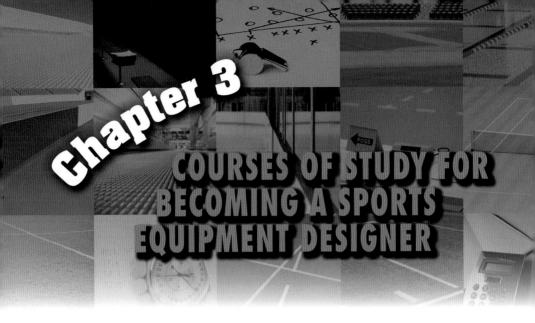

Chapter 3

COURSES OF STUDY FOR BECOMING A SPORTS EQUIPMENT DESIGNER

Because there are not that many university programs that focus entirely on sports equipment design, most people in the profession come at it from another angle—mostly through engineering. Engineers apply science and mathematical knowledge to solve problems or invent new technologies or products. Sports equipment is just one of the things engineers can design.

Although some schools now offer specializations in sports equipment design, it's worth considering that such a degree or specialization will not guarantee you a job in the field. Sports equipment design is a highly competitive occupation, and a degree in general engineering will give you a better shot at finding engineering work in the field of sports equipment design and beyond.

There are also postgraduate programs that focus on sports equipment design, and that is also a good option, according to Dr. David James of the Sports

A background in engineering—particularly but not only in the field of mechanical engineering—is a very practical choice to prepare you for sports equipment design.

Engineering Research Group in the United Kingdom. He says: "I think that a post-graduate qualification (MSc) in sports engineering is a sensible option. Developing your core skills in a technical subject during your first degree allows you to keep your options open, and a post-graduate qualification will enhance and apply your existing knowledge base to the sporting environment."

MECHANICAL ENGINEERING

Mechanical engineering is perhaps the broadest of the engineering focuses of study. Mechanical engineers design and manufacture products and the various components used to create products. This can be

Sports equipment engineering—the same as all types of engineering—begins with an idea on a draft board, and often requires revisiting that idea until it is successful.

anything from a laser to a spaceship, so what mechanical engineers do is quite diverse and broad. It can also, of course, entail designing sports equipment.

A degree in mechanical engineering will teach you the skills you need to apply professionally. According to the Columbia University description of its mechanical engineering program, one will learn how to understand "the forces and the environment that a product, its parts, or its subsystems will encounter; to design them for functionality, aesthetics, and the ability to withstand the forces and the environment they will be subjected to; and to determine the best way to manufacture them and ensure they will operate

WHAT MECHANICAL ENGINEERS ARE DOING FOR SPORTS

In a paper presented at the International Conference on Sports Economics and Vision of London Olympics 2012 at Delhi University, India, researchers Rakesh Vishwakarma and Honey Bhatia described ways in which mechanical engineering applies to sports equipment design, particularly in ways involving new technologies to assess performance. The following are some examples cited in the paper.

Wearable Swimming Technologies:
With the aid of a small wearable device, swimmers can now train on their own in their own pool while still gathering data about their performances, which otherwise had required a coach and a pool that was equipped with special technology to gather this data.

Running Technology:
Systems for analyzing human movement are expensive and usually are based in a lab. Mechanical engineers, according to Vishwakarma and Bhatia's paper, are working on a means to capture information about a runner's performance, including ground contact time, impact, core stability, and sprint-start technique outside of a lab.

Boxing, Martial Arts, and Combat Sports:
In the case of combat sports such as boxing,

the action takes place very quickly, making scoring and judging difficult. With new technology, it is possible to monitor striking and defensive moves faster than by a judge's eye alone.

Racket, Bat, and Ball:
Assessing and monitoring how players of racket, bat, and ball sports (such as tennis and cricket) perform traditionally requires the observation of a coach or trainer. But with advancements in microtechnologies, they can use affordable, small, and lightweight instruments to monitor performance.

without failure. Perhaps the one skill that is the mechanical engineer's exclusive domain is the ability to analyze and design objects and systems with motion."

It's possible to specialize in a particular area of mechanical engineering. The American Society of Mechanical Engineers (ASME) currently lists thirty-six such subareas, from aerospace engineering to renewable energy. Some schools, such as the University of Colorado, do offer special tracks in sports engineering.

According to the BLS, mechanical engineers earn good salaries, and industries that pay particularly well include oil and gas extraction as well as information services.

Among the top-ranked schools for mechanical engineering are the Massachusetts Institute of Technology (MIT), Stanford University, the University of California, Berkeley, and the University of Michigan.

ELECTRICAL ENGINEERING

Electrical engineers focus on new technologies and work on projects involving computers, robots, mobile telephones, navigation systems, and wiring and lighting systems. In terms of sports equipment design, the skills of an electrical engineer are extremely important. With the availability of new technologies, smart systems for assessing performance and movement are becoming more common.

An interest in understanding how things are built and how that process—and the materials used—can be refined is key to sports equipment design.

Lightweight, wearable equipment in particular is making it easier to gather data without bulky equipment or without affecting the natural environment or movement of the athlete.

Smart technology in sports is in high demand and will likely remain so for a long time coming, as new technologies emerge continuously making more and more devices for performance tracking possible.

According to the Bureau of Labor Statistics, the average annual wage for electrical and electronics engineers is quite strong.

Among the top-ranked schools for electrical engineering are the Massachusetts Institute of Technology (MIT), Stanford University, the University of California, Berkeley, and the University of California, Los Angeles.

BIOMECHANICAL ENGINEERING

Biomechanical engineering applies the principles of mechanics—this can include statics, the study of objects in constant motion or at rest; dynamics, the study of objects in motion with acceleration; kinematics, the study of the motion of bodies with respect to time, displacement, velocity, and speed of movement either in a straight line or in a rotary direction; and kinetics (the study of the forces associated with motion, including forces causing motion and forces resulting from motion).

HOW TECHNOLOGY CAN HELP PREVENT INJURY

In hockey, as in other sports, technology is increasingly used to track data related to athletic performance in order to enhance or improve it. Technology is also used to help prevent injury.

In the National Hockey League (NHL), for example, special technology invented by the Australia-based company Catapult is being used to reduce injuries to soft tissue, including the groins of players. Researchers found that 35 percent of all injuries in hockey occur in those areas and wanted to find a way to reduce this number.

The technology used is able to track the movements of players during hockey games and to determine the impact on the bodies of the athletes. The 3.5-ounce (99-gram) device slides into a pouch worn under the shoulder pads of the hockey player and tracks how quickly the player is moving and how much force is sustained when the player is hit by another player. It can even assess which leg is working harder during play. The device can also help trainers assess how much stress is placed on the groin during play.

Ben Peterson, Catapult's sports performance manager, says, in some cases, coaches and trainers have changed practice plans based on information gathered by the new technology. And he believes the applications of the system will extend beyond injury prevention. "As more coaches see the data and

(continued on the next page)

(continued from the previous page)

understand how to apply it, I believe there is a huge tactical component," he told Sports Illustrated. "What is the load and intensity on guys during a penalty kill? When a work rate rises above X does our penalty kill become less efficient? It will make a difference when (coaches) make better informed decisions about player substitutions and pace of the game."

Biomechanics can be applied to sports in several ways, from analyzing golf swings to enhancing performance to assessing the movements of a figure skater. Biomechanical engineering falls under the broader field of biomedical engineering—applying engineering concepts to health. This is another possible track for a career in sports and in equipment design in particular if you are interested in a career helping athletes recover from injuries, for example.

In 2011, Jennifer Sanfilippo was studying for a graduate degree in biomedical engineering, specializing in sports medicine. "I became interested in sports medicine when I was in high school," she told asme. org. "Participating in sports myself, in the off season, I would stay involved helping the school's athletic trainer

If your interest lies in helping athletes perform at their best and most injury-free, biomedical engineering and sports medicine is a great career choice.

with athletes during the practice season." In college, she began in the biology department, but eventually decided to get a degree in athletic training. "While studying, I had the opportunity to work with various athletes on their injuries," she recalls, "following them to away games, and observing different medical professionals reveal their specific expertise. During this time, I realized my true love of research and my unknown desire to become an engineer."

According to the Bureau of Labor Statistics, the average annual wage for biomedical engineers is high.

Among the top-ranked schools for biomedical engineering are Johns Hopkins University, the Massachusetts Institute of Technology (MIT), and the Georgia Institute of Technology.

PHYSICS

Physics is another broad area of study that has many subareas of focus. In general terms, a physicist is someone who studies how the world works. Many astronomers are physicists, and there are also nuclear physicists, for example. Studying physics means studying how the smallest of particles function together to form new things. If you are curious about solving the mysteries of the universe, physics may be for you.

So how does this apply to sports engineering or equipment design? The study of force is critical in sports, for one thing. According to *New Scientist* magazine, "Sport is not just about maximising the performance of the athlete, it is also about minimising the energy that is lost as we run, swim or slide through the fluids around us. Engineers now know that understanding the forces that dominate a particular sport is crucial to performing well." By studying where energy is lost and reducing how much is lost, sports engineers can develop equipment and train athletes in ways that keep energy levels high and maximize performance.

According to the Bureau of Labor Statistics, the average annual wage for physicists is high.

Among the top-ranked schools for physics are Harvard University, the Massachusetts Institute of Technology (MIT), and Stanford University.

MATHEMATICS

It's probably obvious what a mathematician does: they create and solve mathematical formulas to solve problems. This can be applied anywhere from space programs to universities and also to sports engineering.

A degree in mathematics prepares you to be an analytical thinker. Gathering and analyzing data is applicable to many math-degree-related careers, including accountants and researchers. In sports, as in other areas, many statisticians—people who

If you've ever wondered whether you'll use the math you learn in school in the future, sports equipment design is a very good way. Your math skills will be key to your success.

gather, analyze, interpret, and present conclusions based on data—have math degrees.

According to Chron.com, sports engineering is one of the best career paths for combining a love of math and athletics: "Sports engineers develop and research technologies for the sporting industry. They deal with the athlete's external environment—their gear, tools, and equipment. They design sporting equipment that improves the athlete's performance. This can include making a race canoe more comfortable or designing a soccer ball to bounce a certain way when the athlete kicks it. They test the athlete's interaction with equipment and then design or improve the equipment to help the athlete achieve better performance. They conduct extensive testing of equipment, assess how rule changes affect the athletes and analyze athlete injuries."

According to the Bureau of Labor Statistics, the average annual wage for mathematicians is high.

Among the top-ranked schools for mathematics are Harvard University, the Massachusetts Institute of Technology (MIT), and Stanford University.

SPORTS MEDICINE

Although there is a difference between sports medicine and sports engineering, the two fields have a lot of crossover. In order to understand what kind of equipment is needed, particularly that which will be used to help heal or prevent injuries in athletes, knowledge about the body and how it works is crucial.

The important field of sports medicine involves health care related to sports and physical recreational activities. A sports medicine degree can give you a background in human kinetics, which is the study of human movement, as well as exercise physiology, which is the scientific study of how a body physically responds to exercise, including changes to the heart. Such knowledge will prepare you for identifying, treating, rehabilitating and preventing injuries.

Within the overarching field of "sports equipment designer" are many specific specializations to focus on, from medicine to technology to nutrition.

According to the Bureau of Labor Statistics, the average annual wage for sports medicine is quite good.

Among the top-ranked schools for sports medicine are the University of Southern California in Los Angeles, the University of Virginia in Charlottesville, and the University of Pittsburgh in Pennsylvania.

SPORTS SCIENCE

A degree in sports science teaches you all about sports performance and the factors that affect physical behavior in sports. The study includes such subjects as physiology (the study of living things and their parts), psychology (the study of the human mind as related to behavior), biomechanics (the study of the laws of movement), and nutrition. The degree provides a large set of skills that can be used in lots of different careers, including sports equipment design.

A degree in sports science can lead to a career in a variety of sports-related professions, including managing a fitness center, coaching a sports team, being an exercise physiologist (treating patients through exercise), or it can help prepare you to consult with sports engineers to help design effective and safe sporting equipment.

The Bureau of Labor Statistics does not provide salary information specific to sports science.

Degrees in sports science are offered at universities including the University of Connecticut, the University of Nebraska-Lincoln, and Georgia Southern University.

COMPUTER SCIENCE

Sports and technology are becoming more and more combined as new smart technologies lead to wearable equipment that can help track and provide data for later analysis of an athlete's performance.

Technology advancements have not only changed how performance can be tracked, but also how scoring is performed and how some sports are played. One of the later sections in this resource describes many of the ways technology has changed and improved sports and helped reduce injury and improve recovery.

An education in computer science will prepare you to help develop and design new technologies to be applied to sports, be it in equipment design, sports medicine, application of technologies from other fields of study (for example, to help develop new fabrics or materials to be used to design sports equipment).

According to the Bureau of Labor Statistics, the average annual wage for computer science professionals is quite strong.

Among the top-ranked schools for computer science are the University of California Berkeley, the Massachusetts Institute of Technology (MIT), and the California Institute of Technology.

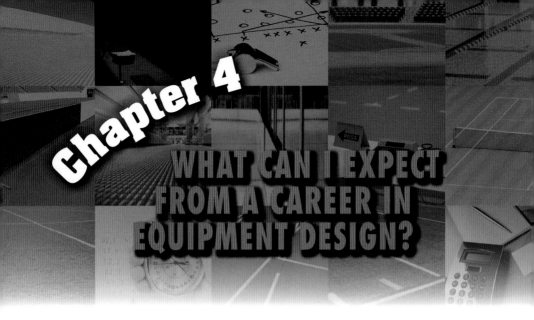

Chapter 4

WHAT CAN I EXPECT FROM A CAREER IN EQUIPMENT DESIGN?

S ports equipment design is a broad field that offers a variety of work environments and roles. It can entail working as a researcher in a university or for a multinational equipment manufacturer. In general, sports equipment designers test equipment (for motion analysis or impact) and build prototypes to be used in these tests. They also assess the human body to figure out ways to prevent injury or improve performance.

The materials used to make equipment also have to be designed—including new lightweight materials or ones that can withstand greater impact. And more and more, sports equipment designers are working on technical innovations—hardware and software—to aid in performance.

People often confuse the role of a sports scientist with that of a sports engineer. The two professions do have a lot of overlap, but they are not the

In the field of sports equipment design, one important aspect is to consider how the athlete will use and interact with the equipment being designed to help reduce injury.

same. A sports scientist is more concerned with the athlete—how much oxygen he or she uses, his or her diet, which muscles are being worked the most. A sports engineer focuses on how an athlete interacts with equipment. The two overlap in the field of bio-mechanics, where sports engineers create systems to analyze an athlete's movement. Sports scientist then use that data to develop ways to improve the athlete's performance.

HOW THE WAFFLE IRON INSPIRED THE FIRST NIKE SHOE

In the 1960s and 70s, as running became increasingly popular as a means of exercise, sports equipment manufacturers began looking for ways to improve the running shoe.

In 1971, an inventor and track coach named Bill Bowerman was having breakfast with his wife. Bowerman

As with any scientist, designer, or other creative professional, inspiration can come from the most unlikely places—even the breakfast table.

was trying to come up with a solution to a problem: how to develop a running shoe that would be lighter and faster. Specifically, he wanted a shoe that had no spikes but could grip easily on artificial surfaces.

"It was one of the few (footwear-related) things he ever talked to me about, so it was kind of fun for me," his wife told Nike historian Scott Reames in an interview he did for Nike in 2006. "I picked out a couple pieces of jewelry and things that had stars on them, or things that we thought would indent or make a pattern on the soles. We were making the waffles that morning and talking about (the track). As one of the waffles came out, he said, 'You know, by turning it upside down—where the waffle part would come in contact with the track—I think that might work.' So he got up from the table and went tearing into his lab and got two cans of whatever it is you pour together to make the urethane, and poured them into the waffle iron."

While creating his prototype for the shoe, Bowerman destroyed the waffle iron, but he soon received a patent for his idea. He began selling the shoe with his business partner Phil Knight, and eventually they formed a company that became Nike. This idea led to the Nike Waffle Trainer, which was released in 1974 and quickly put Nike on the map as a leader in sports shoe design.

One very positive point about a career in sports equipment design is there is no end to innovation and improvement—equipment can always be refined and tweaked to function better.

WORKING FOR A MAJOR SPORTS EQUIPMENT COMPANY

Big multinational companies such as Nike and Adidas hire engineers to work on the design and testing of all levels of equipment. Jobs such as these are very competitive, so landing one can take time and a lot of networking.

Bigger companies producing sports equipment in a large market—such as running shoes—are more likely to offer a higher salary than smaller companies focusing on very specific, smaller markets.

Large sporting goods manufacturers who conduct testing on a myriad of running

THE PHYSICS OF BALLS

For ball sports—football, baseball, golf, and the like—physics can tell sports engineers a lot about how a ball will act during play. Physics can tell us how a ball will travel through the air and how it will spin, for example. Physicist Michio Kaku describes how the stitching on a baseball impacts the ball on bigthink. com:

"We all know that when you look at a baseball, it has threading woven through the leather of the ball in a particular shape. The threads of each section meet at the seam of the opposite thread on the other side of the cut. Tests, including time-lapse photography and wind-tunnel technology, have allowed us to determine that these threads play a huge role in the success of the fastball, curveball and even the famed knuckleball. Basically it boils down to: The faster a ball spins as it slices through the atmosphere, the more stable it is from point A to B. Since a fastball spins very rapidly for example, it is very stable and this is widely due to the layout of the threading."

Kaku also references an experiment done by researchers at Arizona State University to test the performance of golf balls in various weather conditions. "One of the battery of tests they performed took 64 high-powered computers running for a full week to evaluate the flight of one ball under one set of conditions," he says, illustrating how much work goes into testing and analyzing sports equipment.

shoes are likely to pay much more given their market share than a company that specializes in niche sports or smaller markets.

The Bureau of Labor Statistics classifies sports equipment engineers as materials engineers, and the average pay is high.

WORKING IN A LAB

Sports engineers can also be researchers, working at universities or other research facilities to develop and test materials. There

As a sports equipment designer, you may find yourself working with athletes or you may find yourself working in a laboratory, testing and refining ideas.

are also large companies that create materials for all uses, including sports equipment. WL Gore, the innovators behind Gore-Tex, is one example.

At Washington State University, there is a lab that is entirely focused on bat and ball performance for baseball and softball. In the United Kingdom, a company called Sports Labs tested Goal Line Technology systems for soccer—a system that can detect when the ball has crossed the line and a goal is scored. Several professors in MIT's Department of Mechanical Engineering have worked on the design of America's Cup sailing boats.

Research conducted at the University of Southampton's Performance Sport Engineering Laboratory (PSEL) in the United Kingdom helped the British earn Olympic gold in cycling in Beijing, Vancouver, and London, thanks to the RJ Mitchell wind tunnel used in performance testing.

Chapter 5

RECENT INNOVATIONS IN SPORTS EQUIPMENT DESIGN

Technology has enabled a vast amount of improvement in the sports equipment available to professional athletes and amateurs alike. The clothing we wear is not only getting more comfortable, with the invention of new fabrics, but it's also getting smarter, with the availability of technological devices that can be worn to track heart rate, oxygen flow, and pacing.

Even in recent years, the advancements that have been made in sports equipment design are impressive. This chapter covers just a few areas of sports equipment that have been enhanced or forever changed through innovative sports equipment designers.

TECHNOLOGY TO IMPROVE PERFORMANCE

Technology has driven the advancement in sports equipment design. Many technical advancements have

Technology is the latest frontier in sports equipment design innovation. With the use of apps, sensors, and other tools, equipment is getting "smarter."

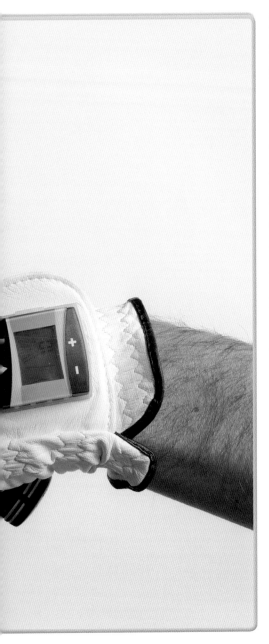

helped improve the performance of athletes and the equipment they use.

In golf, for example, the SensoGlove, a glove worn by golfers, helps players calculate the effectiveness of their grip on a club. It has four tiny sensors sewn into it that read the user's grip pressure eighty times a second. The readings are then read by a computer and the results appear on a small LED monitor on the back of the glove.

In basketball, the 94Fifty is a smart ball equipped with a sensor that helps the player improve shooting technique. Such "smart" equipment is being developed constantly to help a player better refine his or her play and achieve greater success.

WHO WORE IT BEST: WHEN CLOTHES MATTER MOST

Innovation in clothing and material design is also boosting the performance of athletes. Materials that are referred to as reactive respond to the body's temperature and perspiration. To keep an athlete dry and to reduce chafing of the skin, moisture-wicking material doesn't absorb sweat like other fabrics, but instead moves it to the surface where it can evaporate.

Other fabrics and materials include, thermal fabrics which react to body temperature and keep the body warm in cold conditions. Compression

Sports equipment design extends beyond what athletes use to play sports to include what they wear, and what difference that can make to performance.

fabrics tighten around the muscles being used in a workout to maximize performance.

Smart clothing, as its known, uses technology to track or boost performance. There are, for example, socks that can record speed and weight distribution and socks that work like a pedometer, tracking distance as the wearer walks or runs.

For example, an article published in *Ergonomics in Sport and Physical Activity* describes the research that discovered that body suits cause less drag than traditional suits in competitive swimmers.

Developing sport-friendly clothing takes a lot of research, just as it is with creating any other sports equipment. A research paper called "Ergonomic considerations for sports clothing" describes a study that led to a conclusion about swimwear:

The design of swim clothing has progressed from traditional trunks for male competitors and single (one-piece) suits for females. [Researchers] measured passive drag at different towing speeds during starts and push-offs in a swimming pool. They concluded that it is possible for body suits that cover the torso and legs to reduce drag and improve performance of swimmers. [A later study] demonstrated that swim performance over six distances from 25 to 800 m was improved by 3.2% on average when normal swimwear was replaced by a full-body or waist-to-ankle fastskin suit."

WHAT TECHNOLOGY HAS MEANT FOR GOLF

Although innovations in technology and new equipment have improved athletes' performances in all sports, there have been sometimes unexpected consequences. Over the last twenty years, there have been significant advances made in golf equipment. Improvements to golf clubs have made it easier for players to hit the ball farther and straighter, for example. The clubs are lighter, but the head of the driver is also larger than in previous decades. Putters have become more balanced. Even the balls have changed. The number of layers used in manufacturing the ball can impact the distance the ball will travel.

Golf shoes have improved significantly from earlier models, making them lighter, waterproof, and more comfortable as you walk an eighteen-hole course.

Range finders use laser technology to determine how far a golfer is standing from a hole, which has the advantage of helping the golfer pick the right club to make a more precise shot.

The result of these new technologies and equipment is golf players are getting better than those from earlier generations, and now golf courses played on for major tournaments are becoming too easy. With all the improved training and playing equipment, it's a challenge for some older golf courses to stay difficult enough for top-level players. Augusta National Golf Club, home of the Masters, a major golf tournament, has been through one hundred changes since it was built in the 1930s, including changing the grass to make faster greens, and narrowing the tee shot landing area.

KEEPING THE WEIGHT OFF

Lighter materials can mean greater performance and lower chance of injury. Graphite, magnesium, titanium, and advanced aluminum alloys, for example, are widely used in golf clubs, tennis racquets, and racing bikes.

Carbon-fiber composites, which were originally developed in the aerospace field, have been used to produce things from football shoulder pads to skis. It's a material that is durable—it can withstand a high level of tension, impact, and weight—and it is both light and strong.

"Carbon-fiber composites have taken over the sports world in a big way," according to Kim

The application or discovery of alternative materials used to make sports equipment has also boosted the performance in sports from cycling to tennis.

Blair, vice president of operations at Cooper Perkins, Inc., in an interview with Assemblymag.com. Blair has been involved in designing equipment including baseball gear, bicycles, golf clubs, and helmets. "They allow engineers to create optimal strength and stiffness in key locations. A lot of rigidity in sporting goods is governed by tube shape and wall thicknesses. Composites allow us to create more complex shapes and contours."

Skis, for example, have evolved a lot in the last decade, largely due to the availability of new materials. These materials allow them to be incredibly maneuverable and agile on the slopes. Skis need to be lightweight but also resilient—they need to be able to bend and flex on the slopes. Bikes have also changed significantly. "Fifteen years ago, a bike used in the Tour de France race was 20 pounds," says Blair. "Today, you can go down to your local bike shop and buy something that weighs just 15 pounds."

HOLDING IT ALL TOGETHER

With sports equipment engineering, every detail counts, including the adhesives used to keep equipment together. Welding, gluing, or taping in a way that is effective but still visually attractive is something that has to be worked out at the development level.

In the world of sports equipment engineering, every detail matters, right down to the adhesives used to hold pieces of equipment together during manufacturing.

IS ALL THIS ASSISTANCE ETHICAL, OR DOES IT LEAD TO UNFAIR IMBALANCE?

In the original, ancient Olympic games, according to the SportJournal.org, athletes competed nude and all shared the same equipment. There was really no advantage given to one athlete over the other in terms of technology or clothing.

Sports engineers are mostly concerned with improving the performance of an athlete or team. They are also concerned with safety and injury prevention, and work directly with professional athletes to discover a new way to give an advantage through innovation in equipment development. For nonprofessional athletes, sports equipment designers compete for commercial market share, so they look for ways to make equipment better, lighter, smarter, and more effective.

With all the incentive to create new technology and equipment, there's the question of how ethical or fair is it to give such advantages to some athletes.

Technology doping, as it's known, is the use of new technologies to enhance an athlete's competitive advantage. Regulations and rules relating to equipment that can be used in competition on the Olympic, college, and professional level aim to balance the playing field, but can also stand in the way of new inventive designs and technologies.

There has even been controversy regarding artificial limbs used by athletes with disabilities, and whether they give these athletes unfair advantages over non-disabled athletes. Anette "Peko" Hosoi, of MIT, says it's an ethical question that will need to be considered carefully. "Medical technology is good enough now that we can enhance athletes' bodies in ways that

Sports equipment for all types of games and activities has evolved considerably over the years thanks to the efforts and creativity of sports equipment designers.

could give them an unfair advantage over the competition," she says on MIT's engineering website. "People with artificial limbs can now run as fast as able-bodied athletes. It will come down to policy and regulation as to what is allowed, and what isn't, in professional sports."

Looking at every detail of a piece of equipment and applying scientific knowledge to solve problems is a big part of a sports equipment designer's job. No detail can go unexplored.

Anette "Peko" Hosoi is a professor of mechanical engineering at the Massachusetts Institute of Technology (MIT). She mixes sports with multiple engineering approaches, including aerodynamics, heat transfer, human factors, thermodynamics, and vibration, which are applied to help sports equipment manufacturers improve products. Working with a fish reel manufacturer that wanted to reduce production costs, she recommended die-cast parts of the reel be replaced by plastic ones.

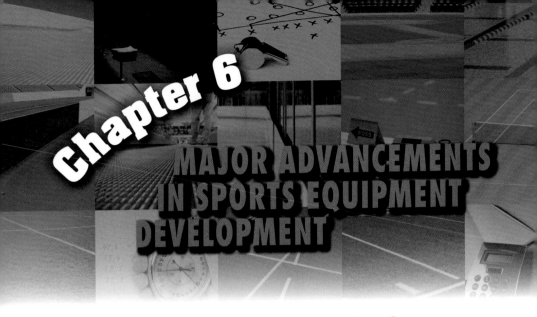

Chapter 6

MAJOR ADVANCEMENTS IN SPORTS EQUIPMENT DEVELOPMENT

Sports engineers are continuously looking for ways to refine equipment and improve how sports are played—reducing injuries, finding ways to have higher-scoring competitions that are more interesting to play and to watch. There is endless potential for advancements in the sports equipment design field.

Innovation in sports is always possible, so the field of sports equipment design is one that should have a long future in front of it. There is no end to how equipment can be refined, improved, replaced, or rebuilt, so the more curious you are as a scientist and the more ambitious you are at identifying and solving problems related to sports, the more you can be sure there will always be work for sports engineers.

Scientists are experts at looking at how things currently are and finding ways to improve on them. Sometimes a change may be quite simple but have long-reaching results that were not anticipated, changing the way a game is paced, played, or scored. Other times the arrival of new materials for building equipment or producing athletic clothing can dramatically improve the performance of an athlete.

The impact sports equipment designers have had on the world of athletics historically has been great. Going forward, there is no way to predict how technology will further advance what equipment we use and what clothing we wear while engaging in sports and how we will analyze our performance and improve on it, as well as how we will prevent and recover from injury.

This chapter describes some of the innovations in sports exercise equipment and engineering during the past two centuries and why they were so impactful to sports. This is just a sampling of the types of results that can be reached with the combination of problem identification and solving, technology, love of sports, and scientific knowledge. This chapter describes several examples of innovations in sports history, as compiled by Complex.com.

THE SHOT CLOCK

The shot clock is mostly associated with basketball, but it's used in other games as well, such as snooker, a vari-

New inventions in sports equipment design can improve safety and performance and even make the play of a sport more exciting.

ation of pool. Introduced in 1954, the shot clock was created to help the game of basketball be higher scoring and more exciting, as the sport was struggling to reach mass audiences and become a mainstream sport.

Before the shot clock, games were low scoring because players would simply hold the ball and let time run out, making it a very dull event for spectators. The shot clock is a timer, which gives players twenty-four seconds to make a shot. The National Basketball Association (NBA) has had this twenty-four-second limit since the 1950s; and college basketball for both men and women has a thirty-second limit.

TITANIUM GOLF CLUBS

Introduced in 1990, golf clubs made of this lightweight material enabled golfers to have a faster swing. Golf club designers have used a variety of material to try and create clubs that improve the accuracy and distance of a drive, which has had a big impact on the game. According to the *Financial Times*, "In 2011, the average drive on the PGA tour in the US was more than 290 yards. In 1980, only six players averaged more than 270 yards."

IN-HELMET HEADSETS

First appearing in 1994, in-helmet headsets allowed for easier communication for quarterbacks. With this invention, quarterbacks can now speak to their coaches via radio. In 2008, these headsets were also permitted between a defensive player and the coach.

The helmets, although in use in professional football for two decades, are still not permitted in college football. Houston coach Tom Herman told *USA Today* he'd like to see that changed. "The immediate advantages would be being able to communicate with my quarterback in the middle of a drive. That's really cool," Herman said. "And to be able to tell him things other than just what play we're calling, even if he's just hearing my voice or (offensive coordinator) Major Applewhite's voice saying, 'Hey, calm down,' giving him some form of instruction in the middle of a drive, I think is pretty critical."

Technology advancements applied to sports and sports equipment have made the equipment used a more important and useful factor in how some sports are played.

COMPOSITE TENNIS RACQUETS

Until composite tennis racquets debuted in 1980, players were still using cumbersome, heavy wooden racquets. Composite racquets are not only lighter than the wooden-framed predecessors, but they have a larger hitting surface and made it possible for players to hit the ball harder.

Today, racquets are made with slightly different materials, but the arrival of the composite racquet changed the game of tennis dramatically.

BETTER RUNNING SHOES

Shoe manufacturers are constantly looking for ways to develop running shoes that give an edge to athletes. In 1951, for example, a Japanese runner won the Boston marathon wearing a running shoe with a special compartment for his big toe.

GOAL-LINE TECHNOLOGY

Used in hockey since first being introduced in 1994, goal-line technology uses a camera above the net so the referees can immediately refer to an instant replay and determine whether the puck crossed the line into the net. In soccer, the technology was not used until the 2014 Brazil World Cup.

LZR SWIMSUITS

According to Complex.com, 98 percent of the swimmers who won medals at the 2008 Olympics were wearing LZR swimsuits, which first appeared the same year. World records were being broken throughout the sport. According to the *New York Times*, in the Olympic individual events, "only four world records remain from the pre-2008, pre-[LZR] era: the men's 400- and 1,500-meter freestyles, and the women's 100 breaststroke and 100 butterfly."

Made of spandex, nylon, and polyurethane, the suits were deemed unfair in 2009 and are no longer permitted in competition.

KERS

Introduced in 2009, the kinetic energy recovery system (KERS) is used in race cars to boost acceleration. It collects and stores kinetic energy—energy an object has from its motion—during braking and releases it during acceleration.

From most lightweight running shoes to the mechanical systems of the fastest racing cars, sports engineers continue to revise and improve every aspect of sports equipment.

BIKE GEARS

Before their invention in 1937, cyclists had to get off of their bikes in order to switch their wheels, depending on whether it was an uphill or downhill segment of a race. Bikes with gears were first used in the 1937 Tour de France.

BREAKAWAY RIMS

These rims, first used in basketball in 1978, are able to bend down when a player dunks the ball. Before their invention, players sometimes broke the rim while dunking, which would delay the game and potentially injure the wrists of the player.

HOCKEY HELMETS

It's hard to imagine playing hockey without protecting your head, but before 1979

Some equipment that just seems so necessary and obvious today—such as the helmet worn in the very injury-heavy sport of professional hockey—was introduced far later into the game than you might expect.

National Hockey League (NHL) athletes were not permitted to wear helmets. Numerous head injuries finally brought about a change in this policy.

CARBON-FIBER SKIS AND SNOWBOARDS

Skis and snowboards have evolved over the years from bulky wooden versions to lighter-weight models. In 1990, carbon-fiber skis and snowboards appeared and became a favorite of the top free skiers and snowboarders.

HAWK-EYE AND CYCLOPS MACHINES

Introduced in 2006, hawk-eye and cyclops machines use cameras and ball-tracking technology to more accurately assess where a tennis ball lands on the court. Their implementation has made it easier to resolve disputed calls.

A CONTINUING NEED

As the sports industry continues to grow and thrive, so does the need to continue to update sports equipment and technology. The latest trends, growing safety concerns, and every athlete's will to succeed will continue to give rise to this exciting industry.

Harvard University
Admissions and Financial Aid
Agassiz House, 5 James Street
Cambridge, MA 02138
(617) 496-0256

Massachusetts Institute of Technology
Admissions Office
77 Massachusetts Avenue
Cambridge, MA 02139
(617) 253-3400
Website: http://web.mit.edu
Programs of study: Chemical engineering, biological engineering, computer science and engineering, bioengineering

Stanford University
Office of Undergraduate Admission
Stanford University
Montag Hall
355 Galvez Street
Stanford, CA 94305-6106
Website: http://www.stanford.edu
Programs of study: Bioengineering, mathematics, mechanical engineering, computer science, physics

University of California, Berkeley
Office of Undergraduate Admissions, University of California, Berkeley
110 Sproul Hall #5800, Berkeley, CA 94720-5800
(510) 642-3175
Website: http://www.berkeley.edu
Programs of study: Materials science and engineering, mechanical engineering, electrical engineering and computer science, physics, mathematics

University of California, Davis
Undergraduate Admissions
University of California, Davis
One Shields Avenue
Davis, CA 95616-8507
(530) 752-2971
Website: http://www.ucdavis.edu
Programs of study: Aerospace science and engineering, biochemical engineering, biomedical engineering, chemical physics

University of California, Los Angeles
UCLA Undergraduate Admission
1147 Murphy Hall, Box 951436
Los Angeles, CA 90095-1436
(310) 825-3101
Website: http://www.ucla.edu
Programs of study: Chemical engineering, materials engineering, computer science and engineering, bioengineering
Website: http://www.harvard.edu
Programs of study: Mechanical engineering, applied physics, mathematics, computer science

University of Colorado, Boulder
Office of Admissions
Regent Administrative Center 125
University of Colorado Boulder
552 UCB
Boulder, CO 80309-0552
Website: http://www.colorado.edu
Programs of study: Applied mathematics, electrical engineering, computer science, engineering physics

University of Massachusetts at Lowell
Undergraduate Admissions
University Crossing
Suite 420, 220 Pawtucket Street
Lowell, MA 01854-2874
(978) 934-4000
Webstite: https://www.uml.edu
Programs of study: Biological engineering, chemical engineering, design and manufacturing engineering, mechanical engineering

Washington State University
370 Lighty Student Services Building
Washington State University
PO Box 641067
Pullman, WA 99164-1067
(888) 468-6978
Website: http://www.wsu.edu
Programs of study: Materials science and engineering, electrical engineering, mechanical engineering, software engineering

Worchester Polytechnic Institute
100 Institute Road
Worcester, MA 01609-2280
(508) 831-5286
Website: http://www.wpi.edu
Programs of study: Biomedical engineering, mechanical engineering, physics, mathematical sciences

SPORTS EQUIPMENT DESIGNER

ACADEMICS

Bachelor's degree (master's degree recommended) in engineering, sports science, biology, computer science, or math

Specialization in sports engineering if available

EXPERIENCE

Interest in sports, particularly if you want to focus on a particular type of sports equipment

Excellent problem-solving and communication skills and a strong interest in science

CAREER PATHS

Sports equipment designer with sports equipment manufacturer

Lab researcher, focusing on materials related to sports engineering

Developer of "smart" equipment used to enhance sporting performance

Teacher at the college level

RESPONSIBILITIES

Design and refine sporting equipment, including clothing and artificial materials on which sports are played

Assist in rehabilitation of people with injuries

Design ways to improve performance through innovations

The Bureau of Labor Statistics classifies sports equipment engineers as materials engineers. Materials engineers are responsible for the design and improvement of almost everything, including sports equipment. Such engineers should have a bachelor's degree, but a master's degree is also recommended, especially if you want to specialize in sports equipment. Because all engineering is about improvement and innovation, the career outlook for the field is very stable. However, sports equipment design is a niche area and very competitive. According to the Bureau of Labor Statistics, "Employment of materials engineers is projected to show little or no change [in the coming decade]. Materials engineers will be needed to design uses for new materials both in traditional industries, such as aerospace manufacturing, and in industries focused on new medical or scientific products. However, most materials engineers work in manufacturing industries, which are expected to experience employment declines."

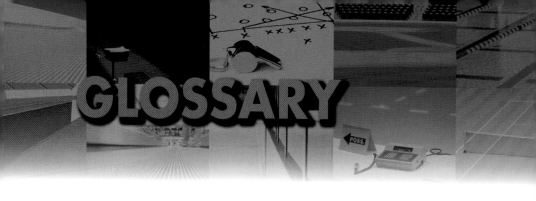

GLOSSARY

adhesives Substances that hold parts of equipment together, such as glue.

aerospace An industry that focuses on designing and building spacecraft.

analytical A problem-solving approach that relies on the review of essential data and how it relates together.

athletic performance The result of an athletic action, including speed, accuracy, and physical health.

biology The study of living things.

biomechanics The study of the impact of outside factors on the physical body.

biomedical engineering The application of engineering principles to the human body, usually related to health care.

CAD Computer-aided design and drafting.

innovative Relating to a discovery or invention that is new and advanced.

kinetics The study of the impact of outside forces on objects in motion.

manufacturer A person or organization that builds products.

mechanical engineering An area of engineering that is focused on the design, construction, and use of machines.

physics A science that deals with matter, energy, motion, and force.

prototype A sample of a product or object intended for testing.

smart clothing Clothing that is equipped with technology.

sports engineer A person who applies engineering knowledge to solving problems related to sports.

sports medicine A medicine discipline that deals with physical fitness and the treatment and prevention of injuries.

sports scientist An area that focuses on the impact of exercise and sports on the body.

STEM Science, technology, engineering, and mathematics.

3D printing A process of "printing" a three-dimensional object via layers.

FOR MORE INFORMATION

American Society of Mechanical Engineers (ASME)

Two Park Avenue

New York, NY 10016-5990

Website: https://www.asme.org

Twitter: @asmedotorg

Facebook: @ASME

ASME is a not-for-profit membership organization that enables collaboration, knowledge sharing, career enrichment, and skills development across all engineering disciplines.

Biomedical Engineering Society (BMES)

8201 Corporate Drive, Suite 1125

Landover, MD 20785-2224

Website: http://www.bmes.org

Facebook: @BMESociety

Twitter: @BMESociety

A society of professionals devoted to developing and using engineering and technology to advance human health and well-being.

Canadian Centre for Ethics in Sports

350-955 Green Valley Crescent

Ottawa, Ontario K2C 3V4

Canada

Website: http://cces.ca

Facebook: @CanadianCentreforEthicsinSport

Twitter: @EthicsInSport

The Canadian Centre for Ethics in Sport works on behalf of athletes, players, coaches, parents, officials, and administrators and serves to elevate the conscience of sport in Canada.

Canadian Sport Institute

100-875 Morningside Avenue

Toronto ON M1C 0C7

Canada

Website: http://www.csiontario.ca

Facebook: @CanadianSportInstituteOntario/

The Canadian Sport Institute Ontario provides programs, services, and leadership to high-performance athletes and coaches.

International Sports Engineering Organization

Broomgrove Teaching Block

Sheffield Hallam University

Sheffield S10 2LX

United Kingdom

Website: http://www.sportsengineering.org

Facebook: @sportsengineeringassoc

Twitter: @Isportsengineer

The International Sports Engineering Association promotes the field of sports engineering through information sharing among its members.

Society of Women Engineers (SWE)

130 East Randolph Street, Suite 3500

Chicago, IL 60601

Website: http://societyofwomenengineers.swe.org

Facebook: @SWEorg

Twitter: @SWEtalk

A society focused on giving women engineers a unique place and voice within the engineering industry.

WEBSITES

Because of the changing nature of internet links, Rosen Publishing has developed an online list of websites related to the subject of this book. This site is updated regularly. Please use this link to access the list:

http://www.rosenlinks.com/GCSI/Design

FOR FURTHER READING

Andrews, Beth. *Hands-On Engineering.* Waco, TX: Prufrock Press, 2012.

Canavan, Thomas. *Fueling the Body.* New York, NY: Rosen Publishing, 2016.

Coles, Jason. *Golden Kicks: The Shoes That Changed Sport.* New York, NY: Bloomsbury Sport, 2016.

Editors of *Sports Illustrated Kids.* *Sports Illustrated Kids Football: Then to WOW!* New York, NY: Sports Illustrated, 2014.

Faust, Daniel. *Building Computers.* New York, NY: Rosen Publishing, 2016.

Faust, Daniel. *Robotic Engineers.* New York, NY: Rosen Publishing, 2016.

Fitzgerald, Theresa. *Math Dictionary for Kids: The #1 Guide for Helping Kids with Math.* Waco, TX: Prufrock Press, 2016.

Graubart, Norman. *The Science of Baseball.* New York, NY: Rosen Publishing, 2016.

Jacoby, Jenny. *Engineering Activity Book.* London, England: b small publishing, 2016.

Kawa, Katie. *The Science of Gymnastics.* New York, NY: Rosen Publishing, 2016.

La Bella, Laura. *Dream Jobs in Sports Fitness and Medicine.* New York, NY: Rosen Publishing, 2013.

Leventhal, Josh. *A History of Baseball in 100 Objects*. New York, NY: Black Dog & Leventhal, 2015.

Lüsted, Marcia Amidon. *Careers for Tech Girls in Engineering*. New York, NY: Rosen Publishing, 2016.

Mahoney, Emily. *The Science of Soccer*. New York, NY: Rosen Publishing, 2016.

Merchant, Raina. *Engineering*. New York, NY: Rosen Publishing, 2017.

Nagelhout, Ryan. *The Science of Football*. New York, NY: Rosen Publishing, 2016.

Nagelhout, Ryan. *The Science of Hockey*. New York, NY: Rosen Publishing, 2016.

National Geographic Kids. *Weird But True! Sports*. New York, NY: National Geographic Children's Books, 2016.

Rohan, Rebecca. *Working with Electricity*. New York, NY: Rosen Publishing, 2016.

BIBLIOGRAPHY

Bachman, Rachel. "Nike's Holy Grail: Bowerman Family Unearths Long-Lost Waffle Iron." *The Oregonian*, February 28, 2011. http://blog.oregonlive.com /behindducksbeat/2011/02/nikes_holy_grail _bowerman_fami.html.

Bhatia, Honey, and Rakesh Vishwakarma. "Mechanical Engineering in the Field of Sports." International Online Physical Education & SportsResearch Journal, April 4, 2012. https://www.scribd.com/document/91795748/ MECHANICAL-ENGINEERING-IN-THE-FIELD-OF-SPORTS.

Bohnett, Charlotte. "Innovative Exercise Equipment for Today's Therapy Clinic." WebPT, June 14, 2012. https:// www.webpt.com/blog/post/innovative-exercise -equipment-today%E2%80%99s-therapy-clinic.

Bond, David. "Will the Goals Start to Flow? The World Waits…." BBC, June 16, 2010. http://www.bbc.co.uk /blogs/davidbond/2010/06/goals_at_a_rare_premium _as_exc.html.

Bruning, Karla. "10 Fitness Fabrics, Explained." *Shape*. Retrieved April 17, 2017. http://www.shape.com/fitness /clothes/10-fitness-fabrics-explained.

Butler, Andy. "Interview with Matt Nurse, Senior Director of Nike Sport Research Lab." October 3, 2014. http:// www.designboom.com/design /interview-with-matt-nurse-senior-director-of-nike -sport-research-lab-10-03-2014/.

Coffin, Phil. "Amid Baseball's Ups and Downs, a Definite

Drop." *New York Times*, September 24, 2011. http://
www.nytimes.com/2011/09/25/sports/baseball/scoring
-in-baseball-returns-to-dead-ball-levels.html?_r=1&.

Collegiate Baseball Newspaper. "Will Flat Seam Baseball
Change the Game?" January 16, 2015. http://baseball-
news.com/will-flat-seam-baseball-change-college
-baseball/.

Columbia University Engineering. "What is Mechanical
Engineering?" Retrieved April 17, 2017. http://
me.columbia.edu/what-mechanical-engineering.

Competitor.com. "BMW Designs New Running Shoes
Using Car Technology." September 21, 2016. http://
running.competitor.com/2016/09/news/bmw
-designs-new-running-shoe-using-car
-technology_155775.

Complex staff. "The Biggest Tech Advancements in Sports
History." Complex, June 4, 2013. http://uk.complex.
com/pop-culture/2013/06/the-20-biggest-tech
-advancements-in-sports-history/.

Daily Mail reporter. "England Players Blame New World
Cup Ball for Green's Howler." DailyMail.com, June 14,
2010. http://www.dailymail.co.uk/news/article-1286255
/WORLD-CUP-2010-England-blames-Adidas
-Jabulani-ball-Robert-Greens-howler.html.

Davoren, Julie. "Careers That Combine Math & Sports."
Chron.com. Retrieved April 17, 2017. http://work
.chron.com/careers-combine-math-sports-24662.html.

Epic Sports. "Baseball Equipment History." Retrieved April
17, 2017. http://baseball.epicsports.com/baseball
-equipment-history.html.

Filingeri, Davide, and George Havnith. "Human
Skin Wetness Perception: Psychophysical and

Neurophysiological Bases." PhD thesis, February 3, 2015. http://www.tandfonline.com/doi/abs/10.1080/233 28940.2015.1008878?needAccess=true.

Gray, Richard. "British Cycling Team Develop New Drag Resistant Clothing and Helmet." *The Telegraph*, November 20, 2013. http://www.telegraph.co.uk/sport /othersports/cycling/10461757/British-cycling-team -develop-new-drag-resistant-clothing-and-helmet.html.

Haake, Steve. "Sports Engineering: The Physics of Sport." *New Scientist*, July 4, 2012. https://www.newscientist .com/article/mg21528722-700-sports-engineering-the -physics-of-sport/.

Hynd, Noel. "The Inside Story About Baseball in 1943 Was Less Bounce to the Ounce." *Sports Illustrated*, May 13, 1985. https://www.si.com/vault/1985/05/13/622451 /the-inside-story-about-baseball-in-1943-was-less -bounce-to-the-ounce.

James, David. "How to Be a Sports Engineer." International Sports Engineering Association. Retrieved April 17, 2017. http://www.sportsengineering.org/students /how-to-be-a-sports-engineer.

Kaku, Michio. "The Physics Behind Ball Design." Big Think. Retrieved April 17, 2017. http://bigthink.com /dr-kakus-universe/the-physics-behind-ball-design.

ME Today. "Biomedical Engineering in Sports Medicine." ASME, August 2011. Retrieved April 17, 2017. https://www.asme.org/engineering-topics/articles/ bioengineering/biomedical-engineering-in-sports -medicine.

MIT, Professional Education. "Advances in Computer-Aided Design for Manufacturing." Retrieved April 17, 2017. http://professional.mit.edu/programs /short-programs/computer-aided-design.

Newcomb, Tim. "Tech Talk: How the NHL Is Using Catapult Technology to Reduce Injuries." *Sports Illustrated*, February 20, 2015. https://www.si.com/edge/2015/02/20/tech-talk-catapult-tracking-nhl-data-injury-reduction.

NOCSAE. "History and Purpose." Retrieved April 17, 2017. http://nocsae.org.

PBS. "Albert G. Spalding." Who Made America? Retrieved April 17, 2017. http://www.pbs.org/wgbh/theymadeamerica/whomade/spalding_lo.html.

Reilly, Thomas. "Ergonomic Considerations for Sports Clothing." Human Kinetics. Retrieved April 17, 2017. http://www.humankinetics.com/excerpts/excerpts/ergonomic-considerations-for-sports-clothing.

Rymer, Zachary D. "The Evolution of the Baseball From the Dead-Ball Era Through Today." Bleacher Report, June 18, 2013. http://bleacherreport.com/articles/1676509-the-evolution-of-the-baseball-from-the-dead-ball-era-through-today.

Shaevitz, Marjorie Hansen. "Everything You Should Know About Applying to and Becoming an Engineering Major." Huffington Post, July 1, 2014. http://www.huffingtonpost.com/marjorie-hansen-shaevitz/everything-you-should-kno_2_b_5548052.html.

Stephens, Laurie. "Why Effective Communication Is Important for 21st Century Engineers." U of T Engineering News, April 28, 2015. http://news.engineering.utoronto.ca/why-effective-communication-is-important-for-21st-century-engineers/.

Stewart, Jack. "The Most Insane Yacht on Earth Just Got Even Insaner." *Wired*, February 14, 2017. https://www.wired.com/2017/02/oracle-americas-cup-yacht/.

Wanucha, Genevieve. "Inside the Fastest Boats in America's Cup History with MIT MechE." Oceans at MIT, August 26, 2013. http://oceans.mit.edu/news/featured-stories /full-speed-frontiers-yacht-design-americas-cup-2013.

Warren, Tamara. "The Yachts of America's Cup Are Faster and Weirder than Ever." The Verge, May 25, 2016. http:// www.theverge.com/2016/5/25/11771276 /americas-cup-boat-design-team-oracle.

Weber, Austin. "New Materials Spur Innovation in Sporting Goods Manufacturing." *Assembly*, November 4, 2014. http://www.assemblymag.com /articles/92480-new-materials-spur-innovation-in -sporting-goods-manufacturing.

Weinswig, Deborah. "The Disruptors of Sports: Smart Sports Equipment." Fung Global Retail & Technology, June 14, 2016. https://www.fbicgroup.com/sites/default /files/Smart%20Sports%20Equipment%20by%20 Fung%20Global%20Retail%20Tech%20June%2014%20 2016.pdf.

INDEX

ABOUT THE AUTHOR

Tracy Brown Hamilton is a journalist who has written several books on young adult nonfiction topics. She lives in the Netherlands with her husband and three children.

PHOTO CREDITS

Designer: Brian Garvey; Layout Designer: Ellina Litmanovich; Editor: Bethany Bryan; Photo Researcher: Sherri Jackson